Rebuilding and Remembering

Kenneth C. Haugk

Journeying through Grief
Book 4

Rebuilding and Remembering
Journeying through Grief—Book 4

ISBN: 1-930445-11-3

Printed in the United States of America.

16
15

Contents

"I will turn their mourning into gladness;
I will give them comfort and joy
instead of sorrow."

Jeremiah 31:13

A Note to You

Nearly a year has passed since you lost your loved one. There may have been times when you wondered whether you could survive without that person in your life. But you have survived, and the wound from your loss will continue to heal.

This is the last of the four *Journeying through Grief* books. My hope is that this book will help you through the one-year anniversary and encourage you as you piece together a new life without your loved one.

Thank you for allowing me to walk with you during the first year of your grief journey. May God continue to provide you with comfort, strength, and healing.

Ken Haugk

It's winter inside,
and I don't know if
spring will ever come.

But every once in a while
I think I see a sprig of green
pushing up through the frozen ground.

Maybe, just maybe
spring will come.

Be with me, God,
while I watch for spring.
Be with me, God,
when the icy winds blow.
Be with me, God,
when I slip and fall.

Help me to endure the winter.
Help me to wait for spring.
Help me to give hope a chance.
Help me to live again.

1

Permission to Grieve—Again

I was talking with a friend who several years earlier had experienced a number of significant losses all within a one-year period. He handled them the best he could at the time, but I could tell he was still hurting. So I asked him how he was coping, and he began to fill me in on how things were going in his life.

It was a good conversation, and I could see how helpful it was for him to talk to someone about his losses once again. But suddenly he stopped sharing—almost in midsentence—and apologized to me: "I'm sorry about going on and on like this in front of you. I didn't mean to have a 'pity party' for myself."

> *Through many dangers,*
> *toils and snares,*
> *I have already come;*
> *'Tis grace hath brought me*
> *safe thus far,*
> *And grace will lead me*
> *home.*
>
> John Newton
> "Amazing Grace"

I was a bit surprised at his reaction. My friend was simply sharing from his heart—in a very healthy way—some of the pain he still had inside. But something

3

caused his social conditioning to kick in, and the myth that he was well beyond the "accepted" grief period led him to feel guilty for talking about his losses and to stop doing the very thing that would help him heal.

What wound did ever heal but by degrees?

William Shakespeare
Othello

I told my friend that there was no need for him to apologize. I had invited him to share in the first place, and I hadn't detected a shred of self-pity. I told him that it didn't matter how long ago his loss was or how many times he had already shared his story. If something was still weighing heavily on his heart, it was healthy—and healing—for him to talk about it.

Some people in your life may treat your loss as if it were ancient history. They may be subtly—or not so subtly—telling you to "get over it" or to "get on with your life." Go ahead and ignore any messages like this. Give yourself permission to grieve for as long as you need to grieve. Your loss has shaken your life, and it takes a long time to pick up the pieces and find a way to put them back together again.

Don't hurry yourself or let anyone rush you. Share the pain of your grief with safe people who will listen to you and appreciate what you have lost. Each time you open up and share, you're letting go of a little more hurt and allowing a little more healing to take place. That's the way grief goes—a little at a time, day by day, for as long as it takes. So give yourself permission to grieve—again.

2

The First Anniversary

For many people, the one-year anniversary of the death of a loved one is a very difficult time. It's common to begin feeling anxious about the anniversary weeks in advance. Some people think and worry so much about the anniversary beforehand that they actually work through a lot of the painful feelings ahead of time. When the day finally arrives, it may not be quite as bad as they had feared. For others, the anniversary is still a very difficult day.

Although anniversaries can be painful, they can also be healing. One woman told me she "made a date" with her deceased husband for that day. She listened to the tape of his memorial service, looked at their picture albums, and read sympathy cards. "I cried and laughed and touched memories I hadn't been able to touch before," she told me. Another woman said she had her mother's wedding ring resized and began wearing it on the first anniversary of her mother's death. It gave her something to look forward to on that day as well as a tangible way to feel closer to her mother. On the one-year anniversary of their son's death, a couple I know planted an azalea bush that would bloom every spring in his memory.

Here are some ideas grieving people have shared with me for handling the one-year anniversary.

• Talk to someone about your loved one on that day. Let one or two close friends or family members know that you'd like to call them on this date and that you need them to listen. Better yet, if you can, get together on that day to talk about your loved one.

• Reach out to others who are also grieving for your loved one. A man told me that he was afraid to talk with his father about the anniversary of his mother's death because he didn't want to cause him more pain. But his father called him on that day to say, "One year ago today your mom died." They opened their hearts to each other; they cried and laughed as they remembered her—and grew closer as father and son.

> *The anniversary date of a loved one's death is particularly significant. You will have done something you thought was impossible a few months earlier. You will have survived an entire year without someone who was as important to you as life itself.*
>
> Bob Diets
> *Life After Loss*

• Do something special to remember your loved one on that day. Light a candle, look at pictures, release balloons or butterflies, plant a tree, place flowers on the grave, tell stories, write a poem, or say a prayer. It doesn't need to be a big ritual. Simply do what is most meaningful and helpful to you. If that means doing nothing special, that's okay too.

• If you feel like crying, let the tears flow. Let them cleanse your heart and heal your soul.

> *Give your burdens to the LORD, and he will take care of you.*
>
> Psalm 55:22 (NLT)

I've also learned that not everyone has a difficult time with the first anniversary. A number of people have told me that for them the anniversary was relatively easy compared to the loved one's birthday or their wedding anniversary. So if you're not anxious about the day, nothing is wrong with you. It's just another example of how everyone's grief is different.

If you start to feel anxious as the anniversary approaches, one of the best things you can do is to tell others close to you what you need and want on that day. A friend of mine knows a woman who lost a young daughter decades ago. Every year the woman and her husband held a small celebration on the child's birthday to commemorate her brief life. No one else knew that they did this—not even their two other children. After her husband died, the woman felt doubly apprehensive as the child's birthday approached. Not only was her husband gone, but she no longer had anyone to share that day with. She told my friend, who encouraged her to tell her two remaining children (now adults) about this tradition and ask them to join her for the ritual this year. She was concerned they'd think it was a peculiar idea, but she told them anyway—and they were deeply touched and very glad to be part of the celebration. It became a new and rich family tradition that deepened their relationship.

The anniversary may be a difficult day, but it doesn't necessarily have to be a bad day. The day can bring back many painful feelings from your loss. But the day can also bring healing as you find ways to remember your loved one, share stories and tears with those close to you, and cherish the special place your loved one will always hold in your heart.

3

The Second Year

There's a myth that the one-year anniversary marks the end of the mourning period. After a year has passed, many people mistakenly think that a grieving person should be over the loss and able to move on with his or her life. In reality, nothing magical happens at the end of one year. You don't go to bed on the 365th day still grieving and wake up the 366th day feeling completely healed. You don't receive a one-year diploma that says you've "graduated" from your grief.

As I said in Book 3, most people will take two to three years to do all the grieving they need to do. Some may take more, and some may take less, because there's no one-size-fits-all time frame for grief. You are unique, and your personal time frame is the only one that matters for you.

What can you expect in the second year? Much depends on the circumstances of your loss, how much time you've actually had to grieve, given everything else going on in your life, how much support you've received from people around you, what other losses you may have experienced before or after this loss, and probably a thousand other variables. But, based on the experiences many grieving people have shared with me, here's what you might expect in the second year.

- **Continuing upsurges of grief.** Waves of painful feelings still come, and some may even knock you off balance. As time goes by these waves come less often, are more gentle, and pass more quickly—but waves will still come.

- **Special days can still be rough.** If the first year was "the year of the firsts," this is "the year of the seconds." You may have expected and even dreaded the firsts. But many people are surprised to discover the depth of their feelings on birth-

> *Grief is like a journey one must take on a winding mountainside, often seeing the same scenery many times, a road which eventually leads to somewhere we've never been before.*
>
> Gladys M. Hunt

days, holidays, and other special occasions in the second year. They wonder, "Shouldn't I be over this by now?" Special days eventually do get better, but some of them may still be surprisingly tough in the second year.

- **Pressure to be "over it."** Much of this pressure may come from other people who mistakenly think you've had plenty of time to grieve. But you may also find that a lot of the pressure may come from yourself. Recognize that you can't grieve according to someone else's expectations or schedule—you will grieve as long as you need to grieve. Accepting your own personal timetable frees you to grieve and heal.

- **Pressure to map out the rest of your life.** For a long time you may have been living day by day, but some of your friends, relatives, and others may be pressuring you to focus on the future and make long-term plans and decisions. Perhaps you are putting some of this pressure on yourself. Unless you need to act quickly for financial, health, or safety reasons, it's perfectly okay to continue to put off long-term decisions and to take things one day at a time if you're not yet ready to look farther down the road.

- **A need to take care of yourself.** It's still quite easy to neglect your own needs—particularly your physical needs—so be sure to get adequate food, sleep, and exercise, and visit your doctor if you have any problems. Take good care of yourself—not only for your own sake, but also for the sake of those who may depend on you and love you.

• **A continued need for support.** Even during the second year, you will benefit from *Healing people*—those caring individuals who are *Here* for you, *Empathetic* toward you, *Accepting* of you, and *Listening* ears for you—especially during times when the waves of grief hit you strongly again. If you have healing people in your life, continue to rely on them. If you don't, seek them out.

As I've said before, grief support groups are wonderful places to find healing people. If you haven't tried one of these groups yet, consider doing so. If you tried one and gave up on it, consider trying again. Sometimes the timing may not have been right, or perhaps it just wasn't the right group for you. Each group has its own personality and focus, so you may need to try a few different groups before finding one that really fits. I can tell you from personal experience, finding the

> *But those who hope in*
> *the LORD*
> *will renew their strength.*
> *They will soar on wings*
> *like eagles;*
> *they will run and not*
> *grow weary,*
> *they will walk and not*
> *be faint.*
>
> Isaiah 40:31

right group is well worth the search. And if you ever feel stuck in your grief or completely overwhelmed—now or at any time in the future—talk with a counselor, pastor, physician, psychologist, or other professional caregiver. Asking for help when you need it is not a sign of weakness; it's a sign of true strength and courage.

A friend of mine told me about a time when he and his brother went hiking in the Great Smoky Mountains. They took a rugged, wooded path that wound its way back and forth up the side of a mountain. Every once in a while, they'd reach a break in the trees and could see the peak of the mountain far above them—but it always seemed far away and never appeared to get any closer. After what seemed like hours, they stopped in a clearing to catch their breath, and my friend expressed his frustration to his brother: "We've been hiking forever, but it seems like we haven't made any progress at all!" His brother laughed and told him to turn around and look behind him. My friend was astonished to see a great valley stretching far below them; the path they had hiked for hours was but a slender thread winding its way through the vast forest.

> *The pain passes, but the beauty remains.*
>
> Pierre Auguste Renoir

At times you may feel like that hiker. It's easy to get frustrated when you only look at how far you still have left to go. Healing from the loss of a loved one is a long, rugged journey full of ups and downs, twists and turns, and unknown territories. Be patient with yourself and take the time you need. But every once in a while, when you reach a clearing where trees aren't blocking your view, glance back at where you've been. (If you've been journaling, read through past entries from time to time.) You'll be surprised to see just how far you've come.

> *I trust in you, Lord, but keep helping me in my many moments of distrust and doubt.*
>
> Henri Nouwen
> *Heart Speaks to Heart*

Even if you still have a long way to go, you're making steady progress in your grief journey. And whether or not you feel God's presence in your life right now, God is with you every step of the way.

4

Rebuilding Your Life

A woman whose husband died told me about the time when she first realized she'd turned a corner in her grief: "One day I found myself laughing, and for just a moment I had a glimpse of joy. It was then I began thinking that perhaps—just perhaps—I could make it. Over the next several weeks, the thought kept growing in my mind and gradually changed from 'Perhaps I can make it' to 'I am going to make it.'"

Sooner or later most grieving people reach a point when they begin to spend less and less energy on simply *surviving* the loss and begin to spend more and more time rebuilding their life—often a very different life than the one they had before.

> *Out of my pain, God became a living reality to me as never before.*
>
> Gerald Sittser
> *A Grace Disguised*

In one sense we begin rebuilding our lives the moment our loved one dies. But rebuilding doesn't begin in earnest until we've sifted through the majority of the feelings, memories, and issues that resulted from our loss. Only then do we have the strength and footing to begin putting our whole self back into daily life and looking to the future.

Rebuilding doesn't mean your life goes back to exactly what it was before—life can never be the same because of the loss you've experienced. Rebuilding means picking up the pieces and putting them together again, but probably in a very different way because a significant piece of your life is missing and cannot be replaced.

Rebuilding usually begins to happen slowly. Exactly when this transition starts to take place depends on many variables: What are the timing and circumstances of your loss? What was your relationship to the loved one who died? How much time and energy did you have to invest in your grief during the past year? How much support did you have from others? Many of the people I've talked with said they began rebuilding somewhere between one and two years after their loss. But again, everyone is different.

> *I learned to trust that through God's grace something beautiful and new would emerge even in the face of my weakness, tears, pain, and hopelessness. I too would live again.*
>
> Bethel Crockett
> "Pooky's Triumph"

You may be approaching that transition now, or perhaps it's still somewhere down the road. Either way is perfectly fine. You'll begin rebuilding your life when the time is right for you.

"I will bless you with a future filled with hope."

Jeremiah 29:11 (CEV)

5

Continuing Bonds

"Love doesn't die. Only people do," one grieving mother told me. "I'll always love my daughter and take comfort in the fact that somehow, in some way, she'll always be loving me."

Experts used to say that people who were grieving needed to emotionally disconnect from the person who died in order to move on with their lives. More recent thinking recognizes that the relationship with a loved one doesn't really end—it changes. Part of what we do during grief is to develop a new relation-

> *Death ends a life, but it does not end a relationship.*
>
> Dennis Klass

ship—a continuing bond—in which we don't disconnect from our loved one, but instead *reconnect* with him or her in a new and different way. This doesn't mean that we deny that the person has died or that we act as if he or she is still alive. Indeed we let go of our loved one in a physical sense, acknowledging that he or she is gone and that we can no longer have the kind of relationship we once had. Yet at the same time we hold on to him or her in new and different ways—spiritually and emotionally—through our thoughts, memories, and feelings.

There are as many ways to have a continuing bond with a loved one as there are people in the world, so I can't tell you exactly what this new relationship will be like for you. Your continuing bond with your loved one will be different from anyone else's. I thought it might be helpful, though, for you to hear examples of some of the ways other grieving people have described their continuing bond.

• One man said, "Whenever my family gets together, we share 'Dad stories.' We laugh and cry and relive fond memories together. He's still very much a part of our lives."

> *Death leaves a heartache*
> *no one can heal,*
> *love leaves a memory*
> *no one can steal.*
>
> An Irish headstone

• A woman who lost her husband said, "We are bonded forever through our two sons. As I watch them grow up and become the men we hoped they'd be, I know he's very proud of them. Some days I can look into their eyes and see him."

• A grieving father told me, "Waiting for a flight one day, I looked over my shoulder and saw a boy who was about the age my son would have been had he lived. The boy was looking right at me for a moment. It surprised me that instead of feeling sad, I felt comforted, almost as if my son was there. The warm feeling stayed with me all evening long—it was a gift from God."

> *I have only slipped away into the next room. I am I and you are you. Whatever we were to each other, that we still are.*
>
> Henry Scott Holland
> "What Is Death?"

- A woman described how her grandmother remains part of their Thanksgiving traditions: "We use Grandma's secret recipes to keep her a part of the festivities. We'll say, 'Here, have some of Nana's scrumptious apple pie.'"

- Another man said, "I remember how my grandfather would think, so I use him as an example of how I live my own life. When something comes up, I'll think about what he'd do in that situation. So I really feel I still have his gentle guidance in my life. I also try to pass on his values to my own children. They never got a chance to meet him, but I can let them know what he was like, so he can still be a significant influence in their lives."

- A grieving wife said, "My husband's lounge chair is my special need-a-hug place. I curl up in that seat to feel close to him."

- One man whose wife died sometimes lights scented candles in the evening, just as she used to do. He said, "It helps me feel close to her."

- A grieving mother told me, "When I close my eyes and pray, I can feel my son kneeling and praying right beside me. Prayer has become my link to him."

- A man whose best friend died while they were in college told me, "Whenever I achieve a milestone in my life, I think about him and in that way make him part of the celebration."

- A woman who lost both of her parents in an automobile accident said, "It may sound silly, but when I pray, I ask God to let my mom and dad know how much I still love them and miss them. It comforts me and helps me feel close to them—29 years later!"

- A man whose wife died just a few months before their granddaughter's wedding gave his granddaughter a string of pearls that had belonged to her grandmother. He later told me, "My wife had wanted to be at that wedding so much. When my granddaughter walked down the aisle wearing those pearls, it felt as if in some way she really was there."

[Love] always protects, always trusts, always hopes, always perseveres. Love never fails.

1 Corinthians 13:7–8

Your continuing bond with your loved one may be similar to one or more of these—or completely different. It might not even involve any conscious thoughts or actions on your part and may simply be an occasional feeling of closeness you have in your heart. Whatever it is, it will be unique to you.

Although we'd much rather have our loved one physically with us, it's reassuring to know that we don't have to completely let go. God has blessed us with thoughts, memories, and a love more powerful than death itself. Through these gifts our loved one can forever remain a cherished part of our life.

6

The Challenges of Change

Change is difficult. Change means leaving the familiar behind and stepping out into the unknown. I don't know if anyone likes to do that. One of the most challenging aspects of losing a loved one is that the loss brings about many changes—changes in the way you live and maybe even changes in the way you think. A big part of your journey through grief is adjusting to these changes.

Some of the changes are temporary. The fog of grief, for example, eventually lifts, and you're able to think, concentrate, and remember like your old self. Some of the changes are permanent. The loss may have left a huge hole that affects how you live your daily life, and you are simply unable to return completely to your former way of doing things.

A grieving husband told me, "Sometimes I don't know who I am anymore." He had lost that part of himself that was a husband to his wife, and he was struggling without that part of his identity. Perhaps you've gone from being a "we" to an "I," or maybe you're now a member of the oldest generation in your family. The loss may mean that you now have to redefine the way you think of yourself.

The loss of a loved one can change the dynamics of the entire family. The remaining family members may need to find a new balance as well as take on responsibilities previously handled by the person who died.

You also face the challenge of finding new outlets for the energy and emotions you used to invest in your loved one. They're like a river that's dammed up and can't flow in the direction it wants to go. While you can't replace your loved one, the love, attention, and energy you gave to him or her need new places to go. This may mean deepening existing relationships or making new friends. It may mean starting new hobbies or possibly finding a new occupation or calling in life. For some people, it may someday mean a new marriage. Again, the point isn't to replace your loved one—no one else will

> *Death changes us, the living. In the presence of death, we become more aware of life. . . . It can inspire us to decide what really matters in life—and then to seek it.*
>
> Candy Lightner
> Founder of M.A.D.D.
> *Giving Sorrow Words*

ever fill that special void—but to find new people or activities for the feelings and emotions you used to give to your loved one. The more you once had invested, the more you'll have to reinvest.

Another challenge is that well-meaning friends or relatives may resist some of the changes they see in you. They may not understand that it's impossible for you to be exactly the same person you were before the loss. Or they may want you to change in a different way.

> *The best thing about the future is that it only comes one day at a time.*
>
> Abraham Lincoln

The changes you face because of your loss are challenging indeed. While I can't make those challenges any easier, perhaps I can share a couple of thoughts to encourage you as you confront the changes you're facing.

First, changes don't have to happen overnight—and they rarely do. If you're faced with a change that seems overwhelming or insurmountable, try a very gradual approach. Take it in small steps, little by little, one day at a time. A somewhat introverted man who lost his wife told me how at one point he felt very lonely and isolated. He wasn't sure how to begin making new relationships but began by simply saying hello to the people he passed while walking his dog each evening. After a while the hellos led to brief conversations, and the brief conversations led to some new friendships. In time, the "cold, unfriendly" neighborhood began warming up, and his feelings of isolation melted away.

Second, as bad as the loss was, the changes that result don't have to be all bad. Often growth can occur as a result. One woman described her grief as a cocoon she entered when her mother died—a dark, lonely, painful time, full of fears and doubts. She wondered if she would ever be happy or feel like living again. She told me it took her two years to emerge from her cocoon, but when she did (like a butterfly) she marveled at the beautiful changes within her. Sure, she'd much rather have had

> *For I am convinced that neither death nor life, neither angels nor demons, neither the present nor the future, nor any powers, neither height nor depth, nor anything else in all creation, will be able to separate us from the love of God that is in Christ Jesus our Lord.*
>
> Romans 8:38–39

her mother back—but that wasn't possible. What she did have was a much greater appreciation for her life and loved ones, newfound strength and self-confidence, more empathy and compassion for others, a richer and deeper faith, and warm memories of her mother that would last forever.

As you encounter changes in your life, tackle them in your own way and in your own time. Nobody knows you better than you, so don't let anyone rush you to change or pressure you to become a certain way. Change in the way you need to change—when the time is right for you.

7

Healing through Helping

One of the most significant changes for grieving people happens on the inside.

- A man who lost his wife told me, "I used to just feel sorry for other people when they lost a loved one. Now I have empathy—I know how much it can hurt, and I'm much more willing to be with them in their pain."

- A woman whose brother died told me, "I now know the value of just being there for someone. I know I don't have to try to fix things or explain it all away. I can just be there for them and listen and care."

Nearly every grieving person I've talked with has told me they've become more caring and compassionate with others who experience losses. They know what it's like to lose a loved one and are much more sensitive to other people's needs.

Over the years I've also learned another amazing thing—*when people give of themselves, they also receive.* I've seen this countless times. When someone reaches out and cares for someone else, the person who is doing the caring benefits almost as much as the person who is receiving the care.

The sequence of care is really amazing.

- Those who lose a loved one need people who really listen and care.

- People who have suffered a loss are much more sensitive and caring to others who are hurting.

- When one person gives care to another person, both end up benefitting.

> *Wiping away someone else's tears is sometimes necessary to help us dispel our own.*
>
> Jimmy Carter
> *Living Faith*

This is one reason why grief support groups are so effective for many people. People come to these groups to receive care for themselves. But part of what they do during each meeting is to care for and support each other—and through those compassionate actions they experience healing themselves.

My fear in writing this chapter was that people could possibly get the wrong impression about reaching out to others. Some might look at it as an obligation—an assignment—they need to complete in order to feel better. Or they might throw themselves into helping others as a way of avoiding their own painful feelings. But neither of these motivations would be good for their own grief journey.

Look to your heart for your motivation. *When you are ready and when you feel it deep inside,* reach out to help someone else who may need it. How you do it—whether calling someone, sending a card, writing a letter, or some other action—depends on what's comfortable, natural, and meaningful to you. It doesn't have to be big or magnanimous; look for even a small way to reach out to someone else.

> *For it is in giving that we receive.*
> St. Francis of Assisi

Not only will it be a godsend for the other person, but you might find it brings healing to you as well.

A father I met at a conference may have said it best. His son had died a few years earlier, and he now takes the opportunity whenever he can to relate to other parents who lose a child. He said, "Helping others won't bring my son back or take away all my pain. But every time I see someone else experience a little healing, I feel a little bit of that healing again myself. It helps to see some good coming out of my sorrow."

8

Rebuilding Is Not Abandoning

A woman who had a stillborn baby described one of the most meaningful and healing encounters she had in her grief. After church one day, an older woman whom she hardly knew pulled her aside, gave her a warm hug, and quietly said, "I've never told anyone about this, but 37 years ago I had a baby who was stillborn, and I want to assure you of one thing. You will never forget— I promise you—you will never forget your baby. He is your baby, and you are his mother. You will remember him always."

The woman said that these words were especially freeing for her because one of her deep-down fears was that she would someday forget her baby. That fear kept her clinging to her sadness, afraid to let go of her grief. But she now knew that she could go on in her life without abandoning her baby. He would always hold a special place in her heart.

Some people resist rebuilding a new life because they're afraid to let go of their sorrow—fearful that letting go means forgetting or dishonoring the memory of their loved one. If they laugh or have fun again, they feel guilty, as if they can keep their loved one's memory alive only by living a life of sorrow.

One woman said, "If I felt even a bit of happiness, guilt would overwhelm me. I thought it meant I was forgetting my dad." A man told me, "Sometimes I felt that letting go of my grief would mean letting go of my son, and I never wanted to do that."

> *What we have once enjoyed and deeply loved we can never lose, for all that we love deeply becomes a part of us.*
>
> Helen Keller

Rebuilding a new life does *not* mean you've abandoned or forgotten your loved one or that you don't love him or her anymore. You don't have to choose between living again and remembering your loved one. He or she will always have a cherished place in your heart. So give yourself permission to live again. To laugh again. To enjoy life again—without feeling guilty. Living again affirms your loved one, who would want the best for you.

A woman described it to me this way: "After my mother died I was sad for a long time. Then I realized that the best way I could honor her would be to try to live with the positive attitude she had and to instill in my children the unconditional love and the appreciation for life that she taught me. In that way her legacy can live on for generations."

"I [the LORD] am with you and will watch over you wherever you go."

Genesis 28:15

9

Healing Memories

Memories are like Greek theater masks—a frowning face and a smiling one. Your memories of your loved one can frown and be painful. But they can also smile and bring comfort and warmth. Both faces of memories are blessings that help in healing.

One fear people have about memories is that they will always hurt, always lead to tears or pain. While it's true that certain memories may hurt sometimes, the pain gradually lessens, and over time the warm, comforting memories can outweigh the sorrowful ones.

If some of your memories are still very painful, let yourself experience them anyway. Don't try to run away from them—as if you could. Just like difficult feelings, the best way to take the sting out of painful memories is to recognize, accept, and express them. Share your memory

> *When you are sorrowful look again in your heart, and you shall see that in truth you are weeping for that which has been your delight.*
>
> Kahlil Gibran
> *The Prophet*

with a trusted friend, talk about your feelings as they surface, and let your tears and emotions flow. You may need to talk about the painful memory—and the feelings it stirs up—more than once. Each time, it will lose a little of its power over you.

> *With love that is almost joy*
> *I remember them:*
> *Lost, and all mine, all*
> *mine, forever.*
>
> John Hall Wheelock

At the same time, tap into happier memories. Look through your photo albums. Remember birthdays, holidays, vacations, celebrations, quiet times, milestones. If you like journaling, write about the good times. Describe special moments to a trusted friend. Exchange cherished stories about your loved one with others close to you. The more you talk about the good memories, the more power they will gain.

One woman told me that a turning point for her came when she sat down to make a scrapbook of her mother's life. "Looking through the old pictures helped me relive many happy memories. I was able to see her as a young wife and mother. That helped me begin to forget the memories of her illness and to finally celebrate her entire life."

People sometimes worry they'll forget their loved one. That person will always be a special part of you, and memories help keep it so. As one woman told me, "Memories are my connection to him. Whether they make me laugh, smile, or cry, they keep him close to me." Another said, "Mom's in my heart now; she goes with me wherever I go."

Sharing memories with others can multiply the healing. One man described how he and a number of his aunts and uncles gathered at his father's grave on the first Memorial Day after his death. They brought folding chairs and sat there for hours, telling story after story. The man heard tales about his dad growing up that he had never heard before. He said, "I went home that day feeling closer to my dad than ever before—in a different way. I had a whole new set of memories to hold on to."

> *Even the saddest things can become, once we have made peace with them, a source of wisdom and strength.*
>
> Frederick Buechner

Memories hurt, memories help, memories heal.

10

God's Aloha

A treasured family photo sits proudly on a shelf behind my desk. It's of my wife Joan, myself, and our two daughters, Charity and Amity. The photo was taken at a luau on a trip to Hawaii, and the backdrop is one of Hawaii's awe-inspiring sunsets.

This photo means more to me with each passing year. It was taken at the sunset of Joan's life—and what a beautiful life it was! Though it marks an ending, it's also a sign of hope and new beginnings for me. The sun never sets but that it also rises to start a new day. And it's that new day that I'm waiting for.

You see, I believe I haven't seen the last—or the best—of Joan. One day I will finish my own journey on earth as she did, and as I stand before God, there she will be too, only better than I ever remembered her—radiating the glory and goodness of God who made and loves us all. Then, I believe, I'll understand completely for the first time what love really is. I'll see how our love for each other on earth is but a reflection of the real thing— in the same way a photo of a Hawaiian sunset can never match being there and seeing the colors paint sky and sea, highlight her hair, and shine in her eyes.

So too, I believe, it will be for you and your loved one. Your grief is real. The pain of your loss is real. The sun has gone down on one who gave your life joy and meaning.

But that's not the end of the story. In God's book, endings are always the preludes to new beginnings. Part of the beauty of every sunset is that it gives us hope for a new day.

> *"He will wipe every tear from their eyes. There will be no more death or mourning or crying or pain, for the old order of things has passed away."*
>
> Revelation 21:4

In Hawaii, instead of saying "good-bye" or "hello," people say "aloha." Aloha both bids farewell and welcomes. Aloha also means love and affection—the kind that doesn't just come and go but endures through all our hellos and good-byes. So I close these four books with aloha—with love and affection for you, my grieving friend.

Aloha—in your good-byes, your losses, your tears.

Aloha—in your hopes and dreams for the future.

Aloha—in your laughter, your loves, and your life.

Aloha—God loves you and holds you in the palm of his hand.

Aloha—God will one day welcome you home and reunite you with your loved one and all who've gone before you.

Aloha—until we meet again in that day with no pain and suffering, but only God's light and love in us and around us forever.

Aloha!

Thank You

I want to thank all those who have given life to this book by opening their hearts and sharing their stories with me at conferences and workshops, in conversations and letters. And I want to thank you, too, for allowing me to walk with you during this time. I will be deeply gratified if you have found some comfort and practical help in these four books.

Because everyone's story is different, I'm always happy to hear from readers like you. If these books have touched you in some way, or if you have any insights about grief that you'd like to share, please write to tell me about your own experiences. May God continue to walk with you.

About the Author

 As a pastor and clinical psychologist, Dr. Kenneth C. Haugk has counseled and cared for many people grieving the loss of a loved one. As the founder and executive director of Stephen Ministries, he has devoted his professional life to helping congregations train their members to minister to those who are grieving or struggling with other life difficulties.

His ministry took on deeper significance as he dealt with the death of his wife, Joan, in early 2002 after a three-and-a-half-year war with ovarian cancer. In putting together the four books comprising *Journeying through Grief,* Dr. Haugk writes from the heart, drawing from his professional work, his own personal experiences, and what he has learned from others who are grieving.

Dr. Haugk is the author of numerous books and is a nationally known speaker and educator. He has received the National Samaritan Award from the Samaritan Institute for significant contributions to the field of caring ministry.

About Stephen Ministries

Stephen Ministries is an international not-for-profit Christian educational organization based in St. Louis, Missouri. Since 1975, it has provided Christ-centered training and resources to over 12,000 congregations from more than 170 denominations. Stephen Ministries publishes books and conducts seminars on a variety of topics, including grief, lay caregiving, dealing with cancer, spiritual gifts discovery, assertiveness, spiritual growth, leadership, and crisis care.

To learn more about our ministry and resources, contact us at:

Stephen Ministries
2045 Innerbelt Business Center Drive
St. Louis, Missouri 63114-5765
(314) 428-2600
www.stephenministries.org